Henry F. Gillig

Hints

To the American Traveler abroad

Henry F. Gillig

Hints
To the American Traveler abroad

ISBN/EAN: 9783337292423

Printed in Europe, USA, Canada, Australia, Japan

Cover: Foto ©Andreas Hilbeck / pixelio.de

More available books at **www.hansebooks.com**

HINTS

— ·:)·:·❮ "HINTS" ❯·:·⋗: —

TO THE

AMERICAN TRAVELER ABROAD.

CORDNER BROTHERS & COMPANY, PRINTERS,

32 HAWLEY STREET, BOSTON, MASS.

Every line in this publication is "original" and compiled expressly for and by the author and is the experience of a ten years' residence (1869 to 1879) abroad as Manager of the Information Department of the late firm of Bowles Bros. & Co., and later, as Founder, Proprietor and Manager of THE AMERICAN EXCHANGE AND READING ROOMS, 449 Strand, London.

FUNDS.

—o—

N leaving the United States, the best, or at least the most convenient, "funds" to take with you are :

1st. A Sterling (English money) Letter of Credit.

2d. About £5 in "Sovereigns" (English gold) for one person, £10 for two or three, £15 for four to six, etc. This will be ample for your fares from Liverpool to London, and until you locate at your hotel or boarding-house, after which you can draw upon your Letter of Credit at the house whose name you will find indicated thereon. If inconvenient to call upon the house indicated, there are other "institutions" which will cash your "letter," and your hotel proprietor *may* know how to do it.

As a general thing a sterling "letter" is better than one in francs, even though you use it mostly on the continent, as the "exchange" is generally in favor of England, and you will get more for your draft on London in every country in Europe, Asia and Africa— excepting, possibly, France—than if you draw upon a letter of credit issued in francs, on Paris.

BILLS OF EXCHANGE.

If you intend remaining in any one country for any considerable time, it is cheaper to have your agent at home send you bills of exchange from time to time, as you may require. But be sure to have such bills mailed at least three weeks before you will require the money in England; if on the continent, at least four weeks; and always have duplicates of said bills forwarded by the next mail after the originals have gone. Much trouble and suffering arises among Americans in Europe from delay of remittances. This is generally the plea of the impostor, but very often of the entirely trust-worthy but timid and mortified traveler, who is obliged to apply to his banker or an unknown fellow-countryman for aid to bridge over the "delayed remittance" time. On this account it is advisable to take with you a small Letter of Credit, payable in sums as drawn, to be used only in the above emergency. (Of course there *are* parties in whose hands such a letter would be also an "emergency.")

Where two or more persons are traveling together, always have the Letter of Credit or Bill of Exchange made out payable to *either of two* at least, as otherwise death or accident may leave the party temporarily penniless.

Note Carefully. — If Mr. John Smith wishes to send a Bill of Exchange to Mrs. Smith, *don't* have it made payable to the order of Mrs. *John* Smith, but to that of Mrs. Temperance Jane, or whatever may be HER Christian name; and Mrs. Smith, in endorsing the bill, should never use the prefix *Mrs.* The same as regards *Miss* Polly Smith. Always *endorse* your bill with the name *exactly* corresponding with the *order* — that is, if the bill reads "to the order of *Mrs. Jane Smith,*" endorse it "Jane Smith;" if to "Mrs. J. Smith," endorse simply "*J. Smith.*" This applies to all documents made out "to order," and non-compliance with such requirements causes frequent annoyance to all concerned.

In all countries, save England, be sure to have your pockets, at the time of your leaving them, as empty as possible of their currency, as you are sure to be "shaved" if you part with it across the line.

For ready reckoning, one pound is called the equal of five dollars, and one shilling, twenty-five cents. •Five francs is called one dollar. The facts are that one pound was never worth five dollars (gold), nor five francs one dollar. Act of Congress made the par value of a pound $4.866, but this is liable to fluctuation according to the temporary balance between the two countries. When you see quoted simply "Exchange on London, $4.86," it means that this is the price at which bankers in the United States are selling a bill drawn by them on a London bank or banker, payable sixty days after it is presented to those London bankers.

If you wish a bill payable at sight (that is, when you call for the cash upon it), the banker issuing it will charge you from one-half to one per cent. more than for a sixty day bill. This would make your pound cost you (with sixty-day bill at 4.866) 4.866 plus one-half per cent. .0243, (=4.8903]; or plus one per cent., .04866 (=$4.9146). The above is for a Bill of Exchange bought in the United States.

——o——

LETTERS OF .CREDIT.

———

Now for your Letter of Credit. The issuing banker will charge you, in the first place, for any sums drawn against it, at the rate of a sight bill. Then he will add one per cent. for his commission. Then he will again add interest from the time you obtain the cash on it (wherever you may draw it, in Great Britain, Ireland or Europe. etc.) to the time at which the money is supposed to be returned to the person in England upon whom the Letter of Credit is drawn—which is generally about thirty days. This will be about one-half per cent. more. equal. at say $4.90 per pound, to .0245.

EXAMPLE.

	£	s.
You draw in London on Letter of Credit, .	100	0
Commission at 1 per cent.	1	0
Interest, 30 days at 6 per cent.—½ per cent.	0	10

Bill presented to your agent in U. S. . £101 10

On receiving this bill from the party who issued the credit in the United States, your agent pays it at current rates of sight exchange, say $4.90 per pound— $497.35—thus making your pound cost you $4.9735.

On account of the commission of one per cent. the Letter of Credit is more expensive than a Bill of Exchange: but when you are traveling from country to country, constantly varying the currency, and liable to lose or be robbed of cash, the Letter of Credit is infinitely to be preferred, as it is payable to you only, and you can use it in sums to suit.

Should you take Letters of Credit for £1000, or upwards, or perhaps £500, I would advise dividing the amount into two Letters of Credit, and keep but one committed about you. What you might lose in "tone" with certain correspondents upon producing a "trifling Letter of Credit" (!) you might gain in not being inconvenienced by losing your dependence. This "division" (or multiplication) of the Letter of Credit is also convenient in case of temporary separation of the party. You may have "business" in Paris (as is likely when

it is very foggy in London), and be obliged to leave
your family behind. It is not a bad idea to have Letters of Credit issued by more than one American
banker.

———o———

CIRCULAR NOTES.

There are also issued by some banks and bankers
for the use of travelers what are called "circular notes,"
in sums of from £5 upward. These are on many
accounts very convenient, but are open to the objection
of bulk, and consequent liability to be lost or stolen.
Still they are better than English bank notes, as they
are payable to order only.

So much for Pounds Sterling, which would be per-
fection were it not for their villainous details of shillings
and pence, which the average man, unprefixed by
"English," is too busy to bother his brains over.

———o———

UNITED STATES BONDS.

On some accounts a United States Bond is a handy
thing to have with you, as it is drawing interest though
lying in your pocket, but there is a liability to loss

which does not attach to Letter of Credit or Bill of Exchange, as the latter two are payable to order only. On the 30th December, 1873, the thitherto *assumed par* of 4s. 6d. for the Dollar was changed by the London Stock Board, to 4s.; so that a quotation of, say 96 per cent. in 1873 was equivalent to one of 108 in 1874. Driven to distraction by £, s., d. calculations, distraction drove us to the invention of the following *formula*, (" Patented" Jan. 7th, 1874) :

To find the value of an United States $1,000 Bond (and we believe that nearly all Bonds issued in the United States are now quoted on the same basis) multiply the *integral* part of the quotation by 2, and add 5s. for every *fractional eighth*.

EXAMPLE.

United States Bond quoted at 109½ = £219.

"   "   "   109⅝ = 219. 5

"   "   "   109⅞ = 219.15

You cannot, generally, sell a *single* Bond at better than within ¼ to ¾ of current quotations. We would not advise taking them abroad for sale, but any banker to whom you may be properly introduced will loan upon them at 6 per cent. or better.

In London and Paris United States Bonds are sold "flat"; that is with coupon included; but in other European markets they are sold "so much" for the Bond and the actual accumulated interest to day of sale.

With your pound costing you $4.90 in the United

States, you ought to get about 49 pence (4s. 1d.) per
dollar, and the general ruling figures are from 48¼
pence to 48½ to 49. 48 pence to the dollar is one
pound to five dollars. In small amounts, say 3 to 15
or 20 dollars, brokers generally give you even money,
4 shillings to the dollar. You can generally get a little
more for $20 (gold) and upward. Greenbacks go at
a shade below coupons or gold.

———o———

BILLS ON THE UNITED STATES.

If your Letter of Credit gives out, as it has a habit
of doing under temptation, if you have no bonds, no
greenbacks, no circular notes, no francs, no friends,
"no nothing," your last resort is, or should be, to
"draw on home."

A well and favorably known or well-endorsed party
can easily "raise the wind" by his draft on home at
the rate of (usually) five dollars to the pound, for any
sum under £100 to £200. He can possibly do a little
better. For larger sums he can easily get a better rate.

The Lord help a not well-known or not well-endorsed
party. Consciousness of untold millions in the home
coffers of such may wreathe his countenance with
smiles as he takes his *morning cab* to his much-used
banker's; the evening pityingly shades his *homeward*

walk, and, after from twenty-four hours to a week of mortification and misery, he makes up his mind and mouth to apply to a stranger for advice or assistance. The best thing to do is to cable, if you can raise the necessary pound or two by borrowing, or by a temporary loan of your watch or jewelry to "my uncle."

———o———

THE CURRENCY OF ENGLAND IS

The pound (sovereign, 20s. gold piece) called						$5.00
" ½ " ½ "		10s.		"	"	2.50
" 5 shilling (rare) crown,			silver,	"		1.25
" 2 shillings & 6 pence, half-crown,				"	"	62
" 2 "	-	-	-	-	- "	" 50
" 1 "	-	-	-	"bob"	"	" 25
" 6 pence,	-	-	-	-	- "	" 12
" 4 "	-	-	-	-	- "	" 8
" 3 "	-	-	-	-	- "	" 6
" 1 "	-	-	-	copper	"	" 2
" ½ "	-	-	-	"	"	" 1

and Bank of England notes for 5, 10, 20, 50, 100, 500, and 1000 (and may be more) pounds respectively.

A guinea is 21 shillings—5 per cent. more than one pound. There have been none coined for many years, but they can be purchased of coin collectors. They charge you guineas instead of pounds to quietly get another five per cent. out of you, as the average "white man" don't know one from the other, until he "balances his books."

On leaving England for the continent, after arranging for your ticket to your first continental important stopping-place, change enough of your English money into francs (French) to pay for your lunch, cab fares in Paris or Brussels (French money here) to your hotel, etc.,— say about one pound (equal to about 25 francs) to each person, and if you have much English money over, take it to the continent in notes of the Bank of England—not in gold. The latter is heavy, and you will get a little less for it on the continent than for notes, for one reason—that it costs more to send it back to England, on account of the transportation.

——0——

FRANCS. (FRENCH.)

———

We have occasionally heard "Old England" roundly anathematized for her villainous currency. France deserves to be saved, if for no other reason than her splendid decimal system.

A franc is worth .193 (not quite 20 cents), though for ready reckoning:

A Napoleon (20 franc gold piece) is about $4.00

½	"	10	"	"	"	2.00
¼	"	5	"	"	"	1.00
5 franc			silver,		"	1.00
2	"			"	"	.40
1	"			"	"	.20
½	"	50 centimes,		"	"	.10
1-5	"	20	"	"	"	.04
2 sous 10		"	copper,		"	.02
1	"	5	"	"	"	.01

An English penny-piece and half-penny, and French
2 sous-piece and 1 sous-piece are current in either
France or England as equivalents respectively.

Francs; as to Letters of Credit, Bills of Exchange,
Circular Notes, Bills on the United States, Bonds,
Coupons and Greenbacks, can be treated in the same
way as Pounds Sterling.

Having thus ventilated Funds, we come to the *possibly* important item in the traveler's "outfit," namely:

————o————

PASSPORTS.

In Austria, Russia, Greece, Turkey, Egypt and Por-
tugal, they are *necessary*, and are occasionally "asked
for" in Italy, Spain and Germany; otherwise they are

not absolutely necessary. We have known the circumstance of a Passport being required for admission to certain *special* picture galleries in Rome.

Naturalized citizens of the United States, especially if they speak English with a foreign accent, should always carry one.

An American-born woman married to an *unnaturalized* resident of the United States, is not an "American Citizen," and if traveling abroad, unaccompanied by her husband, her Passport must be issued by the authorities of her husband's country. This feature caused some trouble during the Franco-German war.

In view therefore of possibilities, including complications that are likely to arise in such a nest of Governments as exists in Europe, we would recommend Passports. They can be obtained of the State Department, at Washington, or of any United States Minister abroad, upon proper identification of applicant.

——o——

BAGGAGE.   (ANGLICE, LUGGAGE.)

———

"Light marching order" is the rule. Take as little with you on the steamer — travel with as little — as possible. Your stateroom trunk, should not be over 20 to 22 inches high, to go easily under your berth — You don't wish "Saratogas" dancing around when "she tips!"

In England, first-class passengers are allowed 120 lbs.—2d. class, 100. From London to Paris, 1st. class, 56 lbs. About 5 cents per pound for excess! On the continent, generally, you must pay for every pound, with some exceptions in France.

In making the tour of great Britain, forward all your heavy baggage to your final leaving place, whether for The Continent or home, by "Goods Train," thus saving at least 50 per cent.

——o——

LETTERS AND "CABLE" ADDRESS.

If you intend traveling during the greater part of the time, it is advisable to make London the distributing point of all your letters, and keep your Banker or Agent there posted as to your movements—as whatever plans you may leave home with are liable to change, and you can more readily act in accordance with such change through London, than with home. If your letters be simply re-directed on the original envelope, there will be no additional postage, if forwarded to any country included in the "Postal Union."

On leaving home, be sure to arrange with your Agent some Cypher Code for use in case of Cabling, and register said Cypher address at the respective telgraph offices at home and in London, Adopt some unusual word as your Cypher, and give the Company your address, to which a "cable" signed thus and received by them, is to be forwarded, your banker, agent, or residence, if permanently located. For instance: if you adopt the cypher "Star" and register it with the Companies "Star London," or "Star New-York," will cost you but for two words in addition to whatever words you may add, delivered to your London address. You are not obliged to sign your name in the body of the despatch, where it will be charged for. Your agent will of course know whence the special cypher comes; as will also yourself on receiving such cypher words. You can extend this code to any extent — words representing sentences. The "Key" of this Code is of course known to yourself, and "Agent" (wife, husband, son or other) only.

After having thoroughly settled all these affairs, compose your mind and body, and proceed leisurely to an Agent of THE NEW YORK LIFE INSURANCE COMPANY, and take out a Policy. It will add greatly to the enjoyment of your trip!

STEAMERS.

On following pages you will find particulars regarding the more prominent lines of steamers, some one of which will meet your case exactly. The tabulations of their respective sailings are made merely to indicate the proposed dates. These are liable to change as regards particular steamers, though it is generally intended that the same steamer shall sail from New York and Liverpool, respectively, every fifth week. Keeping this in mind, you can easily fix the time of your chosen steamer. There are also splendid steamers of the Allan Line, running from Quebec and Portland, to Liverpool or Glasgow; also occasional good steamers of the Anchor or Allan Line from Boston to Liverpool, of the French Line from New York to Brest and Havre, of the North German Lloyds' to Bremen, and the Hamburg Line to Cherbourg (France) and Hamburg.

APPROXIMATE OCEAN DISTANCES.

New York to Queenstown	. . .	3,250	miles.
" Liverpool	, . .	3,490	"
" Hamburg	. . .	3,478	"
" Bremen	. . . .	3,428	"
" Havre	. . . ,	3,028	"
" Brest	. . . .	2,962	"

CALENDAR.

	Jan. **1880**	Feb.	Mar.	Apr.	May	June	
Sund.	4 11 18 25	1 8 15 22 29	7 14 21 28	4 11 18 25	2 9 16 23 30	6 13 20 27
Mon.	5 12 19 26	2 9 16 23	1 8 15 22 29	5 12 19 26	3 10 17 24 31	7 14 21 28
Tues.	6 13 20 27	3 10 17 24	2 9 16 23 30	6 13 20 27	4 11 18 25	1 8 15 22 29
Wed.	7 14 21 28	4 11 18 25	3 10 17 24 31	7 14 21 28	5 12 19 26	2 9 16 23 30
Thur.	1 8 15 22 29	5 12 19 26	4 11 18 25	1 8 15 22 29	6 13 20 27	3 10 17 24
Frid.	2 9 16 23 30	6 13 20 27	5 12 19 26	2 9 16 23 30	7 14 21 28	4 11 18 25 26
Satur.	3 10 17 24 31	7 14 21 28	6 13 20 27	3 10 17 24	1 8 15 22 29	5 12 19 26

	July **1880**	Aug.	Sep.	Oct.	Nov.	Dec.
Sund.	4 11 18 25	1 8 15 22 29	5 12 19 26	3 10 17 24 31	7 14 21 28	5 12 19 26
Mon.	5 12 19 26	2 9 16 23 30	6 13 20 27	4 11 18 25	1 8 15 22 29	6 13 20 27
Tues.	6 13 20 27	3 10 17 24 31	7 14 21 28	5 12 19 26	2 9 16 23 30	7 14 21 28
Wed.	7 14 21 28	4 11 18 25	1 8 15 22 29	6 13 20 27	3 10 17 24	1 8 15 22 29
Thur.	1 8 15 22 29	5 12 19 26	2 9 16 23 30	7 14 21 28	4 11 18 25	2 9 16 23 30
Frid.	2 9 16 23 30	6 13 20 27	3 10 17 24	1 8 15 22 29	5 12 19 26	3 10 17 24 31
Satur.	3 10 17 24 31	7 14 21 28	4 11 18 25	2 9 16 23 30	6 13 20 27	4 11 18 25

———o———

SAILINGS OF OCEAN STEAMERS.

GUION LINE.

New York to Liverpool, via Queenstown.

	Montana	Wisconsin	Arizona	Wyoming	Nevada
June . . .	15	22	29	1	8
July . . .	20	27		6	13
August . .	24	31	3	10	17

Rates of Passage,—$60, $80, and $100. Return Trip, $120, $140, $160.
Children under 12 years of age, half price. Infants free.

AGENTS:

New York	. .	Williams & Guion	No. 29 Broadway.
Boston	. . .	J. J. Shanahan	No. 10 Broad Street.
Queenstown	. .	J. Scott & Co.	
Liverpool	. .	Guion & Co.	No. 25 Water Street.

AMERICAN LINE.
Philadelphia (via Queenstown) to Liverpool.

	Ohio.	British Empire.	Illinois.	British Crown.	Indiana.	Lord Gough.	Pennsylvania.	Lord Clive.
MAY	12	15	22	26	29			
JUNE	19	23	26			5	9	21
JULY				3	7	10	17	21

RATES OF PASSAGE.—$70, $80, $90 and $100. Round Trip, $120, $135, $150 and $175, according to location of Stateroom and number of persons therein.

AGENTS:

PHILADELPHIA—Peter Wright & Co., No. 307 Walnut Street.
NEW YORK—   "   "   No. 52 Broadway.
BALTIMORE—   "   "   No. 44 Second Street.
CHICAGO—   "   "   No. 119 East Randolph St.
QUEENSTOWN—N. & J. Cummins & Bros.
LIVERPOOL—Richardson, Spence & Co., No. 17 and 19 Water Street.
LONDON—Keller, Wallis & Postlethwaite, No. 5 and 7 Fenchurch St.

ANCHOR LINE.
New York to Glasgow or London.

	TO GLASGOW.					TO LONDON.					
	Anchoria	Ethiopia	Circassia	Devonia	Bolivia	Trinacria	Alsatia	Utopia	California	Elysia	Victoria
May	S	15	22	29		S	15	22	29		
June	12	19	26		5	19	26			5	12
July	17	24	31	3	10						

Rates of Passage according to location.
To Glasgow, First Cabin, $60 to $80.   Round Trips, $110 to $140.
          Second   " $40.   "   " $75
" London, First   " $55 to $65.   "   " $100 to $120.
Children from 2 to 12 years of age, Half Fare.   Infants, Free.

AGENTS:

NEW YORK—Henderson Bros., No. 7, Bowling Green.
BOSTON—   "   "   " 103 State Street.
GLASGOW—   "   "   " 17 Water Street.
LONDON—   "   "   " 19 Leadenhall Street.

CUNARD LINE.
New York or Boston, to Liverpool, via Queenstown.

		FROM NEW YORK.					FROM BOSTON.				
	Galia	Bothnia	Algeria	Scythia	Abyssinia	Parthia	Atlas	Samaria	Batavia	Marathon	Olympus
June	30	2	9	16	23		5	12	19	26	
July		7	14	21	28	3	10	17	24	31	
Aug	4	11	18	25		7	14				

RATES OF PASSAGE, $80 to $100.   Round Trip, $144 to $180.
Children between 2 and 12 years of age, Half Fare.

AGENTS :
New York—Chas. G. Francklyn, No. 4 Bowling Green.
Boston—P. H. Du Vernet, No. 99 State Street.
Queenstown—D. and C. MacIver.
Liverpool—   "   "   No. 8 Water Street.
London—William Cunard, No. 6 St. Helens Place, Bishopsgate, and
No. 28 Pall Mall.

NATIONAL LINE.
New York to Liverpool via Queenstown, and to London Direct.

	TO LIVERPOOL.					TO LONDON.			
	Egypt	England	Spain	Helvetia	Erin	Italy	The Queen	Greece	Canada
May ..	29			15	22			12	22
June ..		5	12	19	26	16	23		
July ..	3	10	17						

RATES OF PASSAGE.—Liverpool, $50 to $75.   Round Trip, $110 to $120.
    "   "   London, $50 to $60.   "   " $100.

AGENTS :
New York—F. W. J. Hurst, Nos. 69, 71 and 73 Broadway.
Boston—J. J. Shannahan, No. 10 Broad Street.
Queenstown—N. and J. Cummins & Bros.
Liverpool—National Steamship Co., No. 13 Water Street.
London—National Steamship Co.

INMAN LINE.

New York (via Queenstown) to Liverpool.

	May	June	July	Aug.
City of Berlin . . .	8	12	17	21
" Montreal . .	13	17	22	26
" Richmond .	22	26	31	
" Chester . .	29		1	7
" Brussels . .		3	8	12
" New York .				

RATES OF PASSAGE.—$80 to $100. Round Trip $135 to $160.
Children between 2 and 12 years of age, Half-price.

AGENTS:

New York—John G. Dale, Nos. 31 and 33 Broadway.
Boston—J. H. Palmer, No. 3 Old State House.
Queenstown—C. & W. D. Seymour & Co.
London—Eives & Allen, No. 99 Cannon Street.
Paris—A. H. Johnson, No. 5 Rue Scribe.

9.

WHITE STAR LINE.

New York, via Queenstown, to Liverpool.

	May	June	July	Aug.	Sep.
Germanic	15	19	24	28	
Baltic	20	24	29		2
Celtic	27		3	5	11
Britannic		5	10	14	18
Adriatic		10	15	19	23
Republic					

RATES OF PASSAGE. — $60 to $100. Round Trip, $145 to $175.
Children between 1 year and 12 years, Half-price; Infants, Free.

AGENTS:

New York—R. J. Cortis, No. 37 Broadway.
Boston—C. L. Bartlett & Co., No. 115 State Street.
Queenstown—James Scott & Co.
Liverpool—Ismay, Imrie & Co., No. 10 Water Street.
London—   "   "

QUEENSTOWN.

On arriving at Queenstown, have all letters or telegrams for "home" or elsewhere ready for the tug, which comes out to meet you, for the transportation of the mails, and also for any persons who may wish to land at Queenstown. All the Irish and Continental Mails are landed here, and all the English, excepting those for Liverpool. The delay at Queenstown is made as short as possible—generally not over half to three-quarters of an hour.

Travelers will note that Telegraphic Rates from Queenstown to other parts of the British Islands, and to the Continent, may be a little more than the tariff given on page 28.

Sandy Hook to Queenstown, Great Circle, 3250 miles. Queenstown to Liverpool, 240 miles.

On arrival at Queenstown from Liverpool or America, passengers' baggage is subjected to examination by the Custom-house.

LIST OF DUTIABLE GOODS IN GREAT BRITAIN.

Tobacco, 3s. 4d. to 4s. 10d. per lb.	Spirits, 10s. 4d. per proof gal.
Cigars, 5s. per lb.	Liqueurs, 14s. per gal.
Gold Plate, 17s. per oz.	Tea, 6d. per lb.
Silver Plate, 1s. 6d. per oz.	Coffee 1 1-2d. per lb.
Wines, 1s. and 2s. 6d. per gallon	Cocoa, 2d. per lb.

American reprints of English works are liable to confiscation; Firearms also.

If landing at Queenstown, give all baggage not needed till your arrival in London, to the Agent of the steamer, to be forwarded by "Goods Train" to your hotel (if selected) in London; or to the London Agents of the Steamship Company, to be held till your arrival.

From Queenstown and Cork, you can make your trip to the Irish Lakes, Blarney Castle, etc., and thence to Dublin and Belfast.

QUEENSTOWN CONTINUED.

———

Steamer time between Queenstown and Liverpool about 19 hours.

Express Trains leave Queenstown and Cork, for London *via* Dublin, Kingstown, Holyhead, Chester, (the only "walled" town left in England,) Crewe, Stafford and Rugby, as follows:

WEEK DAYS.	No. 1	No. 2	No. 3
Leave Queenstown . .	9. a.m.	11.30 a.m.	9. p.m.
Leave Cork . . .	10.30 a.m.	12.30 noon	10. 6 p.m.
Arrive at Dublin . .	5. 5 p.m.	5.40 p.m.	4. 5 a.m.
Leave " (Westland Row)	6.45 p.m.	———	6.15 a.m.
Leave " (North Wall)	———	7.15 p.m.	———
Arrive at Holyhead .	11.30 p.m.	1.15 a.m.	11.15 a.m.
Arrive at London (Euston Sta.	6.35 a.m.	9.20 a.m.	6.25 p.m.

Time about 19 hours. Fares, 1st. Class 70s.6d.; 2d. Class, 53s.; *not including conveyance between termini in London.*

Passengers leaving Queenstown by the No. 2 train, if not impeded by too much baggage (which can be forwarded to London as below); leave Dublin at 6.45 p.m., the same as if they had been passengers by the No. 1 train, and thus reaching London at 6.45 the next morning.

Passengers leaving Queenstown on Saturday at 11.30 a.m. and 9 p.m. will reach London on Sunday at 9.20 a.m., and 9.30 p.m., respectively.

SUNDAYS.—Trains leaving Queenstown at 9. a.m. and 9. p.m. and arrive at London on Monday at 6.45 a.m. and 6.25 p.m. respectively.

———o———

LIVERPOOL.

———

If you are not detained by low water on the "bar" of the Mersey, 15 to 19 hours from Queenstown should bring you to an anchorage at Liverpool; where

you are met by the tug, which transports you, bag and
baggage, to the Landing Stage. On the tug you will
generally meet the Agent of the North Western Railway, or of the Midland Railway, who will make any
special arrangement for the transportation of a party
of seven or upwards to London.   Make a bargain
with the Cabman, who takes you to Hotel or Railway Station.   He ought not to charge over 1s. 6d.
for two — 2s. for three — 2s. 6d. for four, and 2d. extra
for each piece of "luggage" taken outside the cab. No
charge for inside.   He will generally, get more, and
right here begins *your* special part in the fight between
Capital and Labor(!); which will rage around you, as
its pivotal centre, till you return to that tug; unless
you are "smart" and keep your temper — in which case
Labor will come out a little ahead! It's bound to win,
anyway, with its myriads of "pickets" in the shape of
"cabbies," "waiters," hotel and boarding-house "ex-
tras," &c., &c.   At any hotel, restaurant, bar-room or
the like in the British Empire or Europe, "you are
expected" to give something extra to the "waiter."
The amount of this fee ("Pour boire" in France;
where, by the way, it is positively obligatory) depends
upon the value of the "goods delivered," and whether
you are an American or not. No one gives less than
one penny for anything; on a simple "drink" an Englishman would give 1d. and on a "square meal," of say
from 3 to 5 shillings worth, 3d. An American would
not be better "served" — scarcely so well — a second

time, if he gave 3d. and 6d. respectively! If you adopt
the lower tariff, the chances are, they will take you for
one of Her Majesty's liege subjects—Try it!

Having now landed upon the shores of that Kingdom "upon which the sun never sets"; inhabited by
the Englishman; but inherited by nine-tenths of the
citizens of the United States,—five hours "rail" brings
you to the greatest and grandest city the world ever
held and, (as Miss Kate Field wittily remarks) "upon
which some people think the sun never rises."

———o———

LONDON.

From May to October, (the former, if not indeed
both, included) 360 degrees of Latitude and Longitude
do not include a hamlet, village, town or city more
thoroughly enjoyable than this, THE COSMOPOLIS. Its
Health record, challenges the world. It can duplicate
or equivalent (*v.!*) any Pleasure found on the "foot-
stool" and to its Business, that of the "great" cities of
the world is mere huckstering. Its Weather during the
above mentioned months, is, despite the cant, Frenchy
affectation or bad digestion of its critics, as good as that
of any other less blessed city in existence.

HOTELS.

The Queens'— Fischer's — Long's—Bath—The Albemarle. (All in the neighborhood of Piccadilly.)

Ashley's — Golden Cross — Charing Cross — **Barnett's** (private). (All in the neighborhood of Charing Cross.)

The Langham — **Herring's** (private) American Hotel — (At the head of Regent Street.)

The best "**home**"in London, No. 3 Bedford Place, Blooms-bury Square.

DINING ROOMS.

Holborn Restaurant (6 o'clock, *Music*—don't miss it)—Kett-ner's, 30 Church Street, Soho. Table d' hote 6 to 8. —The Crite-rion—St. James—The Burlington—Cafe Royal—Simpson's.

BANKERS.

Messrs. Baring Bros. & Co., 8 Bishopgate Street [within.]
"   Brown, Shipley & Co., Founders' Court, Lothbury, E. C.
"   McCulloch & Co. 41 Lombard Street.   [Lane.]
"   Morton, Rose & Co., Bartholomew House, Bartholomew
"   J. S. Morgan & Co., 23 Old Broad Street.
"   N. M. Rothschilds & Sons, New Court, St. Swithins Lane,
"   Seligman Bros., Angel Court E. C.   [E. C.]

AMERICAN BANKERS AND THEIR LONDON CORRESPONDENTS.

New York.	Boston.	London.
August Belmont		N. M. Rothchilds & Sons
Brown Bros. & Co.	Brown Bros. & Co	Brown, Shipley & Co.
Drexel, Morgan & Co.	Jacob C.Rogers	J. S. Morgan & Co.
Kidder, Peabody & Co.	Kidder, Peabody & Co.	Baring Bros. & Co.
Morton, Bliss & Co.		Morton, Rose & Co.
Seligman Bros.		Seligman Bros.
S. G. & G. C. Ward.		Baring Bros. & Co.

AMERICAN OFFICIALS IN LONDON.

U. S. Minister, James Russell Lowell.
First Secretary, W. J. Hoppin; *Second Secretary,* E. S. Nadal.
Offices: The Members' Buildings, Victoria Street, S.W.
Consul-General, Adam Badeau. *Vice-Consul-General,* Joshua
Nunn. Offices: Winchester House, 53a, Old Broad Street.
U. S. Despatch Agent, B. F. Stevens, No. 4 Trafalgar Square.

PASSPORTS are issued by the United States Minister, at the Members Building, Victoria Street, Westminister.

EXECUTION OF DEEDS, POWERS OF ATTORNEY, &c., requiring Official seal, are made by the United States Consul General, 53a, Old Broad Street, and in both cases identification is required.

CAB FARES.

Charing Cross, is the radiating point from which the London cab fares are estimated. If you take a cab at any point within 4 miles of Charing Cross, the fare is,

For not exceeding 2 miles . . . . . 1 shilling.
For each mile or part of a mile beyond 2 . . 6d. additional
If hired by time,
Four wheel [Growler] per hour or less - . 2 shilling
Two wheel [Hansom] " " . . 2s. 6d.
and 6d. [G.] to Sd. [H.] extra for each 15 min. over
If hired outside the 4 miles radius,
For each mile or less . . . · . . 1 shilling
If hired by time,
For each hour or less, ... 2s.6d.
and 6d, [G.] -o 8d. [H.] extra for each 15 minutes over
If hired within, but discharged without the 4 mile radius,
If not beyond 1 mile . . . . . . 1 shilling
For each additional mile within the 4 . . 6d.
" " " beyond the 4 . . 1s.
These fares are for either one or two persons.
For each person more than two . . . 6d. additional
Additional children . · . . . . 3d.
Luggage, 2d. each package taken outside.

In hiring by the mile you are at liberty to stop anywhere on the route to your destination, provided that your stop or stops do not exceed 15 minutes in the aggregate—and you can take any route you please provided that the distance gone does not exceed that for which the fare is fixed.

For further particulars [and in fact for everything else in London] see Dickens's Dictionary of London," price 1s.

The Excursion Tickets of Messrs. Cook & Son, offer at least one unquestionable advantage, namely: by taking them, you are saved the annoyance of buying your tickets *with* and *in* the score of different currencies and tongues of Europe.

ENGLISH POSTAL INTELLIGENCE.

RATES OF POSTAGE.

To all parts of the United Kingdom —

Letters, 1 oz. or under, 1d.; Newspapers, 1-2d.
Books, periodicals, photographs, printed or manuscript matter,
etc., per 2 oz. or under 1-2d. Must be open at the ends, and not ex-
ceed 5 lb. in weight, or 18 inches in length. English Postal Cards,
7d. (thin) to 8d. (thick) per dozen.
Registration of letters, 2d. extra.
To European countries, Egypt, and United States per 1-2 oz. or
under 2 1-2d.
Postal Cards, 1d.
"Commercial Papers," (legal documents and other manuscript
matter not of nature of a letter) not exceeding 4 oz.—2 1-2d.
Per two ounces additional 1d.
Books, newspapers, periodicals, photographs, printed matter,
&c., per 2 oz. or under, 1-2d. Must be open at the ends, and not exceed 4lb. in weight, or 12 inches in width or depth, or 24 inches in
length.
Patterns of merchandise, not exceeding 2 oz. 1d. Must not exceed 8 oz. in weight, or 8 in. by 4 in. by 2 in. in size.
Letters can be posted in London, up to 5.50 p.m. at Sub-Post
Offices and Pillar Boxes. At Euston Square Railway Station up
to 8.25 p.m. 2d. extra. Continental letters at Charing Cross Railway Station up to 8.15. p.m. 6d. extra.

TELERAPHIC RATES.

Throughout United Kingdom, 1s. for 20 words; address and sig-
nature, free.
Alabama, Arkansas, Florida, (Lake City, Pensacola, St, Mark's
Tallahassee) Georgia, Indian Territory, Iowa, Kansas, Louisiana,
Minnesota, Mississippi, Missouri' (except St. Louis), Nebraska,
North Carolina, Tennessee, Texas, Wisconsin, (except Milwau-
kee,) 3s. 8d. per word.
Arizona, California, Colorado, Dakotah, Idaho, Kansas. Mani-
toba, Matamoras, (Mex.) Montana, New Mexico, Oregon, Utah,
Washington Territory, Wyoming, 3s. 10d. per word.
British Columbia, Florida, (other than above) Vancouver, 4s.
6d. per word.
Canada, Cape Breton, Connecticut, Maine, Massachusetts, New
Brunswick, New, Hampshire, New York City, Nova Scotia, Prince
Edward's Island, Rhode Island, Vermont, 3s. per word.
District of Colombia, Delaware, Maryland, New Jersey, New
York State, Pennsylvania, 3s. 2d. per word.
Illinois, Indiana, Kentucky, Michigan, St. Louis, Mo., Ohio,
Virginia, West Virginia, Milwaukee, Wis., 3s. 3d. per word.

To Austria 4 1-2d. per word		To Norway 4d. per word	
To Hungary 5d.	"	To Portugal 6 1-2d.	"
To Belgium 2d.	"	Russia in Europe 9 1-2d.	"
To France 2 1-2d.	"	To Spain 6d.	"
To Germany 4d.	"	To Sweden 5 1-2d.	"
To Holland 3d.	"	To Switzerland 4d.	"
To Italy 5d.	"	Turkey in Europe 8d.	"

MAILS FROM AMERICA.

Days of Sailing.	Line.	Due in London.
Tuesday	Guion	Saturday
Wednesday	Cunard	Saturday
Thursday	Inman or W. Star, Hamburg	Monday
Saturday	W. Star or Inman	Tuesday

MAILS FOR AMERICA.

Days of Sailing.	Line.	Close in London.	Close in Paris.
Tuesday	Inman or W. Star	Tuesday	Monday
Thursday	W. Star or Inman	Thursday	Wednesday
Saturday	Cunard	Saturday	Friday

Scotch mails, Saturday from Greenock. Irish, Sunday from Londonderry.

DIFFERENCES IN TIME.

NEW YORK EQUIVALENTS.

Boston	. . . .	12.11.42 p.m	Paris	. . . . .	5. 5.21 p.m
Berlin	. . . .	5.30.15 "	New Orleans	. .	10.55.31 a.m
Cincinnati	, . .	11.18.23 a.m	Philadelphia	. .	11.55.21 "
Chicago	. . . .	11. 5. 9 "	St. Louis	. .	10.43. "
Liverpool	' ' '	4.44. 4 p.m	St. Petersburg	.	6. 4 p.m
London	. . . .	4.55.36 "	San Francisco	.	8.46.23 a.m

Confucius says, (or ought to) that, next to Truth, the mightiest and prevailingest thing is, to hold your tongue, when folks lie like thunder *for* you.

GUIDE BOOKS.

There is a score of good Guide Books — Harpers, Appletons, Murrays, &c., &c., useful and intsructive; but for "light" traveling you can't do better than Houghton, Osgood & Co's "Satchel Guide," and "Badeker's" several publications,—and THIS [!] Don't fail to prqvide yourself with Smith's "Tape" Map of London. Also Dickens's Dictionary of London, price 1s.

RAILWAY TRAVELING.

In hot, dusty weather, you cannot possibly be any more uncomfortable than in, or any "nastier" than when you come out of, a First Class English Railway "Carriage," with its *squshy* luxurious upholstering. TRY 2d. class; 20 to 25 per cent. cheaper. In winter, you run a little less risk of freezing in 1st. class, than in 2d!

PHYSICIANS.

We know it is considered *infra dig*—" against the rules of the R. C. P., &c., &c." for PHYSICIANS to advertise; but DR. THOMAS, (allopath) 15 Weymouth Street, Portland Place, and Dr. YELD-HAM (homœopath) 10 Taviton Street, Gordon Square, will forgive us.

TRADESMEN, ETC.

H. J. SCOTT & SON,
TAILORS,
EXCLUSIVELY TO ORDER.   **55 NEW BOND STREET.**

TRUNKS.
Seller, 23 and 24 Buckingham Street, Strand.

OPTICIANS.
Steward, 406 and 456 Strand.

PATENT AGENTS.
P. H. Justice, [formerly of Philadelphia], 14 Southampton Buildings.

UMBRELLAS.
Martin, 64 & 65 Burlington Arcade, Piccadilly.
Sangster, 140 Regent Street, and 75 Cheapside.

TAILORS.
FENDICK, 67 Strand;
        HAMILTON & KIMPTON, 105 Strand.

CIGARS AND TOBACCO.
John Chandler, Charing Cross Station-gate.

THOMAS COOK & SON,
Tourists' Agents,
LUDGATE CIRCUS, and 445 STRAND.

TURKISH BATHS.
The Hammam, 76 Jermyn Street; The Argyle Baths, Argyle Place, Regent Street

DRY GOODS.
Swan & Edgar; Lewis & Allenby; Peter Robinson; Marshall & Snelgrove; Farmer & Rogers; Whiteley; Waterloo House; (all " A 1.")

SHIRTS, GLOVES, UNDERCLOTHING, &C.
HENRY CROUCH, 34 Strand.

This Table shows the First-class Fares, the *about* Directions and the Distances from London of sundry important points in England and Scotland. Fares (in shillings and pence) precede, and distances follow names. Second-class fares from 20 to 25 per cent. less. Third-class fares from 40 to 45 per cent. less.

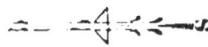

Loch Katrine
Loch Lomond—The Trossachs
Callander
Balloch 60/4—Stirling 420
5S/ GLASGOW 405—57/6 EDINBOROUGH 400
52/10 Melrose 390—54/ Berwick 340
[Belfast] 40/6 Carlisle 300—42/3 New Castle 270
[Isle of Man] 37/ Lake Windemere 260—31/1 Ripon 235—35/ Scarborough 235
39/2 Furness Abbey 260—34/ Lancaster 230—27/6 York 200
29/6 Preston 210—25/9 Leeds 185
[Dublin] 26/9 Bradford 195—28/ Hull 175
29/ LIVERPOOL 200—24/6 Manchester 190—23/ Doncaster 155
43/S Holyhead 264—27/10 Chester 180—19/11 Rowsley Chatsworth 150
24/2 Crewe 160—1 Derby 125—16/9 Boston 110
17/4 Birmingham 115—14/9 Coventry 95
12/9 Rugby 85
15/3 Leamington 95
15/6 Warwick 105
21/ Worcester 120—17/3 Stratford-on-Avon 110
9/3 Cambridge 60—11/10 New-Market 70
11/ Oxford 65
48/3 Milford 285— LONDON
39/ Swansea 215
35/6 Cardiff 170—26/1 Bristol 120—3/9 Windsor 20
15 Southampton 79—17/ Hastings 75
15/ Exeter 170—15/6 Portsmouth 75—12/ Brighton 50—13/9 New Haven 55
46/6 Plymouth 245—40/2 Torquay 220—17/S Isle of Wight 90

15/ Margate 90
15/ Ramsgate 85
20/ Dover 76
Folkstone 70 [Calais]
15/ Canterbury 60
8/6 Tunbridge Wells 35—20/ [Boulogne]
[Dieppe]

COURIERS.

A Courier is a *luxury*. If you can afford one, get a good one, and he will soon become an absolute *necessity*. Get a *bad* one, and you are "done for." Your Banker will, generally, be able to provide you with the address of a good one. Should any *offer* their services, see that their "*credentials*" are all in order.

You *can* get a good Courier, at from £10 to £12 per month, during the *busy* season. A "swell" one will try to get £15. In addition to this amount, you must pay his (2d. class) fares. If the train by which you go, has no 2d. class carriage as is occasionally the case you must pay 1st. class. You do not have to pay his hotel bills; that is, you will not *see* it in your bill! Have your contract with him *in writing* clear and explicit. Give him money enough at starting to purchase railway or other fares, lunches, cab fares &c., and something over, till you are settled at your next resting place. Make him render his accounts every two or three days, and *don't* "skim them over." Don't scrimp him down to the lowest notch. Call him by his surname. A good Courier should know all about your routes, fares, hotels, "sights" etc., and speak English, (*plainly*) French, Italian and German.

TRAVELING SERVANTS

Are not so well posted, and are not expected to take such exclusive charge of your movements and cash, and do not generally "speak all the languages." You can get good (of the kind) for from £6 to £7 per month.

CONTINENTAL MONEY.

With the exception of the currency of France, Belgium, Switzerland and Italy, whose coinage is similar, or interchangeably equivalent those of other European countries are more *crazing* than England's; and Houghton, Osgood & Co's Satchel Guide, (page 286, 1879, Ed.,) will help you out, if anything can.

NOTE CAREFULLY. Where you find gold to be "at a premium," (in Italy for instance) draw gold upon your letter of credit, and sell it to a broker for "paper currency," at the rate of the day, to use in paying your bills; as you get no more at shops, hotels &c., for gold than for "paper." You thereby save the amount of the premium. On leaving countries thus afflicted, have ready the exact amount of your railway fare—otherwise, if the railway makes change at all, you will have a lot of the "stuff" on your hands.

HOTELS IN OTHER PARTS OF THE BRITISH ISLANDS.

CORK, Imperial Hotel. — DUBLIN, Shelburne Hotel.
BELFAST, The Imperial Hotel.

LIVERPOOL.

The Adelphi Hotel. — The Northwestern Hotel.

LEAMINGTON.

Manor House Hotel, E. Duret, Proprietor.

Leamington is the most convenient head-quarters from which to make your excursions to Warwick, Kenilworth, and Stratford-on-Avon.

RYDE, ISLE OF WIGHT.

The Esplanade Hotel, J. Kemp, Proprietor.

EDINBURGH.

The **Windsor** Hotel, 100 Princes Street—opposite the Castle. A. M. Theim, Proprietor.

Grieve's Hotels,—The Balmoral, Royal British and Waterloo.

GLASGOW.

The **Grand** Hotel, Lewis Jefferis, Proprietor.

BRIDGE OF ALLAN.

Philp's Royal Hotel, R. Philp, Proprietor,

LOCH LOMOND.

Inversnaid Hotel, Robert Blair, Proprietor.

MELROSE. •

The Abbey Hotel, G. Hamilton, Proprietor.

We take our *oats* in Edinburgh at brother Thiem's "Windsor," Glasgow, brother Jefferis's " Grand."

During May, June and July, the principal hotels of London, are crowded and it is advisable to secure rooms at least two or three days ahead.

Don't forget the " magnificent" *Coach* rides from the White Horse Cellar, Piccadilly, to Virginia Water, Windsor, Tunbridge Wells, Brighton, etc.

THE GRAND HOTEL, Trafalgar Square, London, was to be opened June 1st. 1880, and if it be what was promised, Americans should take possession at once.

Slouch Hats not current in Lombard Street. — *Stove-pipe* wins every time.

Should you require any Printing in London, Cards, Prospectus, etc., Mr. Shephard, of the Civil Service Printing Co., 8 Salisbury Court, Fleet Street, is your friend. ,

Our London address is care of brother Michell, Ashley's hotel, Covent Garden. *Wait for us there.*

ROUTES TO THE CONTINENT.

SOUTH EASTERN RAILWAY, via FOLKSTONE AND BOULOGNE.

QUICKEST ROUTE TO PARIS.

The time of leaving London depends upon the tide at Folkestone. When leaving anywhere between 7 and 10.45 a.m., this is by far the best route; as it is but 9 1-4 hours to Paris, 255 miles. This is also the only route by which you are accompanied through by an Interpreter. You have but 6 miles more water than

VIA DOVER AND CALAIS.

Which leaves at *fixed* hour, morning and evening throughout the year; but note that the evening train, takes no 2d. class passengers. Time 10 1-2 hours; distance 283 miles.

BAGGAGE.

1st, Class allowed 56 lbs.; over that 2 1-8d. (over 4 cents) per pound. Register all heavy baggage through to Paris. Examination there.

A deck cabin to accommodate from 1 to 6 or 8, can be secured by a telegram to the Superintendent at Folkestone or Dover, a day or two in advance. Price from 20s. to 30s.

The Dover and Calais train takes also the passengers for Brussels, (Belgium) via Calais or Ostend.

LONDON, BRIGHTON, and SOUTH COAST RAILWAY, via NEW HAVEN, DIEPPE AND ROUEN.

Cheapest route to Paris (nearly 50 per cent) and pleasant enough, when you can depend upon the tide at New Haven and Dieppe. Time from 15 hours upward.

The General Steam Navigation Company, and other lines despatch good steamers from the Thames, and via Harwich, to northern Continental ports.

SEA ROUTES.

London to Antwerp	210 miles	Dover to Ostend	68 miles.	
" Rotterdam	230 "	Folkestone to Boulogne	30 "	
" Hamburg	480 "	Newhaven to Dieppe	64 "	
Dover to Calais	24 "	Southampton to Havre	122 "	

EDINBOROUGH.

THE WINDSOR HOTEL,

PROPRIETOR, A. M. THIEM.

LOCATED OPPOSITE THE CASTLE.

☞ Special Attention Paid to American Travelers.

PRICES MODERATE.

Having duly donned the armour of righteousness at St. Pauls, Westminster, etc., you can smile at Satan's rage and face —

THE LONDON MUSIC HALLS,

which *can* afford you much innocent amusement. The best are, the Canterbury, the Metropolitan, the Pavilion, the Royal, and Evans's. Take a reserved seat, a Sangster or Martin umbrella, and one of Chandler's best Havanas.

There is also the Alhambra, a kind of "cross." A Music Hall sired it; a Theater, dam'd it. Havana allowed in "third row" only.

There are also the Discussion Forums, Green Dragon, Fleet Street, and Coger's Hall, Salisbury Court. The Chair sits at 9.30 p.m. Everything in order; from Tobacco and Theology up to Toddy and Treason.

LONDON.

PRIVATE AMERICAN HOTEL,

I5 NEW CAVENDISH STREET, W.

Proprietor, M. HERRING, of New York.

The above establishment offers unrivalled accommodation to Americans during their stay in· London, whether for one day, or for a lengthened period. The situation is in every way desirable, being in the best part of the West End — three minutes walk from Oxford, Bond, and Regent Streets; near the Underground Railway, and convenient to all lines of Omnibusses. all Theaters, Museums, etc.

PARIS CAB FARES.

By the Course	.	.	1 fr. 50	By the Hour	.	.	2 fcs.
	1 honr	2 hours	3 hours	4 hours	5 hours.
	2 fcs.	4 fcs.	6 fcs.	8 fcs.	10 fcs.
15 minutes	2 50	4 50	6 50	8 50	10 50
30 "	3 00	5 00	7 00 ·	9 00	11 00
45 "	3 50	5 50	7 50	9 50	11 50

THE PARISIAN.

A Weekly Continental Newspaper in the English Language.

PUBLISHED EVERY THURSDAY MORNING.

Office, 9 Rue Scribe, - - Paris.

C. S. WASON, Editor.   A. H. JOHNSON Publisher.

Traveler's letters, trunks and packages received and forwarded. All information furnished relative to Paris and the Continent. American papers on file. Open on Sundays from 10 to 12 for delivery of letters.

THE PARISIAN is recognized as the best newspaper in the English language published on the Continent.

Its aim is to give full and accurate information to Americans traveling abroad, and at the same time to entertain people who, having visited Europe, may be interested in the political, literary, dramatic, artistic and social life of the old world.

Bankers do not issue Letters of Credit for less than $500; but will give you Bills of Exchange of, say from £10 to £20 each, for the amount. These are as good as — perhaps better than — Circular Notes.

NEW YORK LIFE INSURANCE COMPANY.

CHARTERED 1841. COMMENCED BUSINESS 1845.

Assets Jan. 1st, 1880, $38,859,830.00   Surplus for Dividends, $7,683,517.00

ADVANTAGES of a Life Insurance Policy over a Four per cent.
United State Bond, or a Savings Bank investment if the insured
dies within twenty-six hours.

AGE 30.

End of Year.	Results of $22.70 a year.		Excess of Profits from the Insurance Policy.	Actual Rate of Compound Interest realized on the Premium Paid.
	Savings Bank with Interest.	Life Insurance Policy, *not counting dividends.*		
1	$23.61	$1000.00	$976.39	4,410 per cent.
2	48.15	1000.00	951.85	2,000 "
3	73.77	1000.00	926.23	350 "
4	100.33	1000.00	899.67	120 "
5	127.80	1000.00	872.20	90 "
6	156.85	1000.00	843.15	60 "
7	185.49	1000.00	813.51	50 "
8	217.55	1000.00	782.45	40 "
9	229.27	1000.00	770.73	30 "
10	283.75	1000.00	716.25	25 "
11	320.07	1000.00	679.93	22 "
12	354.12	1000.00	645.88	20 "
13	392.52	1000.00	607.49	18 "
14	431.30	1000.00	568.70	15 "
15	472.16	1000.00	527.84	13 "
16	515.29	1000.00	484.71	12 "
17	560.69	1000.00	439.31	11 "
18	604.40	1000.00	395.60	10 "
19	652.50	1000.00	347.40	8 "
20	703.43	1000.00	296.57	7 "
21	759.71	1000.00	240.29	6 1-2 "
22	809.72	1000.00	190.28	6 "
23	863.17	1000.00	136.83	5 1-2 "
24	922.12	1000.00	77.88	5 "
25	982.91	1000.00	17.09	4 1-3 "
26	1046.00	1000.00		4 "

(Annual Dividends Paid in Addition.)

In the Last Ten Years.

The New York Life Insurance Company, has paid the following amounts in Cash Dividends to its Policy-holders:—

In 1870 it paid	$1,058,929	In 1875 it paid	$1,369,955
In 1871 "	849,679	In 1876 "	1,409,309
In 1872 "	781,603	In 1877	1,440,936
In 1873	835,637	In 1878	1,555,075
In 1874	1,480,630	In 1879	1,525,340

Total in ten years, $12,313,693

PARENT OFFICE, 346 Broadway, New York.

NEW ENGLAND BRANCH, 131 Devonshire Street, Boston.

R. C. M. BOWLES, Special Agent.

UNITED STATES CUSTOM HOUSE DUTIES.

These be your bounden *duties* *
* dodge them how you may.— *The Smuggler.*

Animals, for breeding purposes	free
" otherwise	20 per cent
Ale, Porter and Beer, in bottles	35 cents per gallon
" " " in casks	20 cents per gallon
Antiquities — not for sale	free
Books — new	25 per cent
" for Colleges, Libraries, or printed more than 20 years, or in use abroad more than 1 year, and not for sale	free
Boots, Shoes	35 per cent
Bronze, manufacturers of	35 per cent
Carpets, Aubusson, Axminster, and all woven whole for room	50 per cent
" Brussels Tapestry, printed on the . . warp or otherwise	28 cents per sq yd and 35 per cent
" Brussels, wrought by the Jaquard . machine	44 cents per sq yd and 35 per cent
" Saxony, Wilton & Tournay Velvet wrought by the Jaquard machine .	70 cents per sq yd and 35 per cent
" Treble Ingrain, three ply, and . . Worsted Chain Venetian	17 cents per sq yd and 33 per cent
" Velvet, Patent or Tapestry, printed on the warp or otherwise	40 cents per sq yd and 35 per cent
Carriages and Clocks	35 per cent
China — Porcelain and Parian Ware, plain .	45 per cent
" Gilded, ornamented or decorated . .	50 per cent
Clothing, wholly, or in part of wool	50 cents per lb and 40 per cent
" Silk component	60 per cent
" All other descriptions	35 per cent
Coral, cut or manufactured	30 per cent
Cutlery, Table, &c	35 per cent
" Pen, Jack and Pocket Knives . . .	50 per cent
Diamonds, and other precious stones, set . .	25 per cent
" Unset	10 per cent
Engravings	25 per cent
Furniture, Furs, manufactured	35 per cent
Gilt and Plated Ware, &c., Guns	35 per cent
Glassware, Gold and Silver Ware	40 per cent
Gloves, Kid	50 per cent
Household Effects — In use abroad one year and not for sale	free
Jewelry — Gold, Silver, or imitation	25 per cent
" Jet and imitations of	35 per cent
Laces, Silk, or Silk and Cotton	60 per cent
" Thread	30 per cent
Linen — Table, Toweling, &c., 30c. or less per sq yd	35 per cent
" Table, Toweling, &c., above 30c. per sq yd	40 per cent
Musical Instruments	30 per cent

U. S. CUSTOM HOUSE DUTIES. (*Continued.*)

Paintings . . . . 10 per cent
" If work of an American Artist . . free
" Frames for do., ... 25 per cent
Photographs . . . . 25 per cent
Pipes — Meerschaum, Wood, and of all other { 1.50 per gross and
    material, except Common Clay . { 75 per cent
Rubber Boots, Shoes, and other articles, wholly
    of Rubber (not fabrics) . . . . . 20 per cent
" Braces, Suspenders, Webbing &c.,
    unless in part silk . . . . 35 per cent
" Silk, Cotton, Worsted or Leather . . 50 per cent
Saddles and Harness, ... 35 per cent
Shawls — Camel's hair, or other wool . . . . { 50 cents per lb, and 40 per cent
Silk — Dress, Piece and Shawls . . . . . 60 per cent
Soap — Fancy, perfumed, Toilet, and Windsor { 10 cents per lb and 35 per cent
Statuary—Marble . . . . 10 per cent
Stereoscopic Views, on glass or paper . . . 30 per cent
Spirits — Brandy, Whiskey, or Gin &c. . . . 2 dls per proof gal
Umbrellas — Silk or alpaca . . . . 60 per cent
Velvet — Silk . . . . 60 per cent
" Cotton, or mostly cotton . . . . . 35 per cent
Watches . . . . 25 per cent
Wines — All *still* wines, such as Sherry, Claret
" or Hock, in casks . . . . 40c. per gallon
" in bottles of 1 pint or less . . . 80c. per dozen
" in bottles of over 1 pint, and less than
    1 quart . . . . 1.60 per dozen
" all Champagnes and Sparkling wines
    in bottles of half pint or less . . 1.50 dols per dozen
" in bottles of over half pint, and not
    more than 1 pint . . . . 3 dols per dozen
" in bottles of over 1 pint, and not
    more than 1 quart . . . . 6.00 dols per dozen
" in bottles of over 1 quart (extra) . 2.00 per gallon

Every person is entitled to one watch of foreign manufacture, and a *reasonable* amount of "*personal effects.*" *All* personal effects in use abroad one year, *free.*

Physicians, Lawyers, Journalists, and professional men, generally, are allowed to bring in certain books, pertaining to their professions, and for their own personal use, *free.*

Surgical and Scientifical Instruments for personal use of party bringing them are also *free.* A Mechanic, also, is allowed to bring in his Tools *free.*

Have your Letters, while in Paris, addressed to THE PARISIAN, 9 Rue Scribe. You can thus obtain them on Sundays, when others are closed.

The Cable Rates given on page 28 are those *generally* charged; but there's no telling how often *the* Company may amuse *itself* by change.

Thanks, old friend KREMER, for remembering us *during our* "*vacation*" by sending us regular file of your Paris *Continental Gazette.*